Coding for Beginners and Kids Using Python

Bob Mather

TABLE OF CONTENTS

Disclaimer

Introduction

Do you want your child to learn coding? I am sure this feels like an impossible endeavor, doesn't it? It is as hard as learning a new language, and this is definitely a daunting experience for a child. It is harder to convince your child to learn to code as well. Every parent has been there. You know how difficult it is to start a new journey. It is quite overwhelming and scary. So, how do you think your child may feel about it? He is going to have a million questions, such as:

- Can I learn how to code?
- Will I ever reach a stage in life where coding is easy?
- When can I use this skill?
- Is it something that will help me in school? If not, why am I even doing it?

These statements stop most of us, so it is going to stop your child, too. The entire process of learning is too tedious. You first need to have a plan in mind, then find the right courses so you learn, make sure you are good enough and then create an app or tool. Having said that, you should first decide what it is you want to learn. You also need to know everything there is to know about the new subject, so you know what the dividend will be. There is no easy way to go about this, and it is a quite challenging task.

A new task may seem impossible when you start off, and it will definitely be hard for you to meet your goals if you do not take the necessary steps. If it is this hard for you, how hard do you think it will be for your child? You need to ensure that you and your child jump in with two feet. If both of you do not commit to learning, it will only lead to frustration. It will also lessen the chance of your child following through with the course and succeeding. It is best to let your child start with something small, take his time to learn and achieve measurable and realistic goals.

If this is what you want to do, you have come to the right place. You will find all the information your child needs to learn more about coding and get involved in it. There are different gamified and fun exercises that will keep your mind engaged. It is quite difficult to engage a young brain and motivate your child to learn something new and complex. However, the information and exercises make coding easy to understand. So, before you coax your child into learning how to code, make sure to do the following:

- Explain to your child why it is important for him to learn to code
- Outline the benefits of coding
- Define some key terms
- Look at different examples
- Choose a programming language and begin!

Coding, in simple terms, is a language used to communicate with computers and machines. You can also use this language to build and run apps, websites and more.

Getting Started

Getting started with coding does not mean your child must make giant leaps. If you read the section above, you know it only means your child needs to start off small. The only thing you must focus on is to ensure your child progresses with every move he makes with respect to coding. This gives rise to the question – why should my kid learn to code?

The idea that kids should lean to code was planted years ago, and at the time, you may have believed it was hype. The concept was new, and every educational institute wanted to include coding classes for kids. The idea was not unfounded, but people needed some time to digest the idea that coding will become the most important strength that people must have. Some statistics show that the number of jobs will increase in the years to come, but the majority of those jobs will be in computing. This makes people wonder if coding is difficult to understand and learn.

Your child should not learn how to code for the wrong reasons. Do not tell him he needs to code to look cool. You must explain to him what the results are and how coding will help him land a good job in the future. Make sure to tell him he will be rewarded if he knows how to code. There are so many jobs out there, and they pay quite well. What makes coding better is that it not only helps your child do well in the future, but it helps him become creative, develop problem solving skills, collaborate with other programmers or people to develop new apps, communicate with them and various other skills that help him become a star employee.

Does this mean learning a new language is as easy as learning how to perform other activities or talking to people? Definitely not. Having said that, it is best to use these reasons to get your child moving if he is wary about learning how to code. Give him a set of guidelines, so he knows where to start. These guidelines will also help him determine where he stands. Coding is the language of the future, and thus it is important for your child to know how to code. As mentioned earlier, when your child learns to code, he also develops other skills that will help him in the future.

Why Python?

What is Python?

When we want the computer to do something, we need to give the computer instructions it can understand, i.e. machine language. Machine Language. Machine Language consists of 0s and 1s. Below is an example of Machine Language:

10011 00011 110001 1001010101 100001 001 0111 0000
11111 11010101

Although the computer might find it easy to read, we humans do not. Therefore, to make instructions readable and easier to understand, we use Programming Languages. We write the instructions for the computer in a programming language, and it is converted to machine language which can be understood by the computer.

Python is an example of a programming language. Below is a piece of code in Python to calculate the average of a student's marks and return their grade base on the average.

```python
def grade(marks):
    sum = 0
    for mark in marks:
        if mark > 100:
            return "Invalid Mark"
        sum += mark
    average = sum/len(marks)

    if average >= 90:
        return "A"
    elif average >= 80:
        return "B"
    elif average >= 70:
        return "C"
    elif average >= 60:
        return "D"
    else:
        return "F"
```

Although you may not know Python, you may be able to understand certain parts of the code. That is the beauty of Python. It's easy to read and understand. Python can be used for various tasks. It can be used to predict stock prices, build software to automate daily tasks, develop APIs for websites, developing games etc. It is actively being used in the field of Machine Learning, Data Science and Web Development. Below is a list of companies that use Python as one of their programming languages

- Facebook
- Google
- Netflix

- Spotify
- Reddit

and the list goes on. Google engineers made the decision "Python where we can, C++ where we must."

Install Python on your computer

1. Go to https://www.python.org/downloads/ and click on the "Download Python 3.x.x". In my case, the latest version is 3.8.4, and since I am on Windows, I will be downloading Python for windows. Make sure you download the latest version of Python for your Operating System.

2. Launch the installer and wait for it to load. Check the "Install launcher for all users". Make sure the "Add Python 3.8 to PATH" is also checked. After you have checked the boxes, click on "Install Now" and wait for the installation to be complete.

3. Once the installation is complete, search for "Python Idle" and start Python.

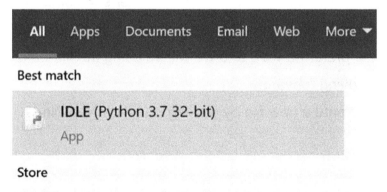

Below is a screenshot of Python idle.

```
Python 3.7.4 Shell                                              —   □   X

File  Edit  Shell  Debug  Options  Window  Help
Python 3.7.4 (tags/v3.7.4:e09359112e, Jul  8 2019, 19:29:22) [MSC v.1916 32 bit
(Intel)] on win32
Type "help", "copyright", "credits" or "license()" for more information.
>>> 8 + 2
10
>>> 1 -3
-2
>>> 1*5
5
>>> 5/3
1.6666666666666667
>>> |
```

Exploring Python

Try typing out a few simple math expressions like the ones above. The window above is called a Python shell, and in the shell, Python gives an output message after each statement. You can also write all your code in a file and run the file using Python, this is the preferred way, and we will be using the file-based coding moving forward.

You can create a new file by clicking on File > New file.

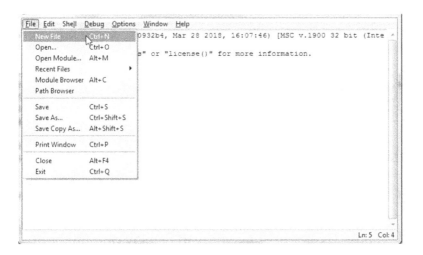

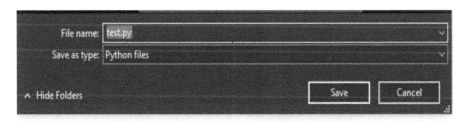

Make sure to save the file with '.py' at the end and the type as "Python files'. This tells the computer that the file contains code which can be executed using Python.

Try typing a few math expressions like in the file. Once done, either press F5 or go the run option and select the run module option. The python shell should open up again, but this time you won't be able to see any output. We need to tell Python to display the output explicitly. We can do so using the print statement, which will be discussed in the below.

13

Python Keywords

1. Syntax

Syntax is to Python what grammar is to English. It is a set of rules that must be followed while writing code. Ex: there is a syntax to display output, there is a syntax to perform complex math functions etc.

2. Comments

Comments are statements which the Python code will ignore. They are used to explain your code to other users, describe the purpose of a particular piece of code etc. The syntax for adding comments is:

```
# Add your comment
```

Python will ignore the line which is preceded by a #

3. Variable

A variable is used to store names or value(s) in Python. Think of it as a box that can value(s). That box is referenced each time you need that value(s). The syntax for defining a variable is as below:

```
var = 10
```

In the above example, var is the name of the variable, and it stores a value of 10. Anytime, you use the name 'var' in your code, Python will replace it with the value, i.e. 10.

The basic types of values a variable can store are:

    String to store text values, ex: var = 'Python is fun'

    Integer to store integer values, ex: var = 10

    Float to store decimal values, ex: var = 9.81

    Boolean to store True/False, ex: var = True

A variable can also store more than one value, and more on that will be discussed later.

4. Function

A function in Python is a set of lines of code with a name assigned to it. A function is used when a certain piece of code needs to be used in multiple places. Instead of typing the lines each time, you can type the function name. When Python sees the function name, it executes the lines of code associated with that function name. First, you have to define a function in the below format:

```
def my_function( input variables ):
        ........ piece of code .........
        return variables
```

A function can take in variables as input known as parameters, do something with the variable such as increasing it by 20, multiplying it with 4 etc. and return the result. The 'return' keyword is used to return a result. In the above case, the name of the function is 'my_function'. A function doesn't necessarily take parameters and return an output all the time, e.g.:

```
def new_function():
        ......... piece of code ........
```

The above is also a valid definition of a function. Python comes with a broad set of pre-defined or built-in functions which are available for us to use, eg: print(), min(), max() etc.

When we want to use a function, we simply invoke it like this:

```
my_function( input variables)
```

If the function doesn't take in any parameters, we do not type anything in between the parentheses. If we expect the function to return a result, we need to store the result in a variable :

```
var = my_function()
```

In the above line of code, we assume we have already defined a function named 'my_function' which doesn't take any parameters but returns a result. This result is stored in the variable 'var'

5. Print

print() is a built-in function in Python. It takes a string, a variable or a combination of a string and variables as its input parameters and displays it on the python shell. Below are some examples:

```
print(.' Python is Fun')  # Prints 'Python is Fun' in
the python shell
print(8+10) # Prints 18 in the python shell

# below are two variables name and age to store
the Name and Age of a
# person
name = 'Peter Parker'
age = 29
print(' My name is {} and my age is {}
years'.format(name , age)
# Prints 'My name is Peter Parker, and my age is
29 years' in the shell
# To print a variable we replace the variable with {}
in the string and use
# .format() function with the variable as the
parameters. The order matters
# and values are replaced respectively
```

```
# Takes in variables name and age as parameters
def my_function(name , age):
    # Increases age by 10
    new_age = age + 10
    # prints output
    print("Hello {}, your new age is {} years".format(name , new_age) )


n = 'Captain America'
a = 90

# calling my_function with above variables
my_function(n,a)

# calling my_function with new values
my_function('Peter Parker' , 20)
```

We have used all the keywords discussed above in this particular piece of code. Function 'my_function' takes name and age as parameters, increments age by 10 and displays it on the python shell. The result from the first function call and the second function call is

```
Hello Captain America, your new age is 100 years
Hello Peter Parker, your new age is 30 years
>>>
```

When writing code inside the function, the code needs to be indented, i.e. a tab space must precede each line of code. Any line not preceded by a tab space will not be part of the function. Ex: In the above code, the declaration of variables n and a are not a part of

Function my_function.

19

The Input Function

To make a program interactive, we need to get input from the user.

To take input from the user, we use the input() function. More often than not, we store the input in a variable, below is the syntax for the statement:

name = input("Input your name")

Example

```
def func(color):
    print("Your favorite color is {}".format(color))


c = input("What is your favorite color? ")
func(c)
```

In the above code, we first ask the user for their favorite color and then pass the color as a parameter to the function func(). func() prints the statement "Your favorite color is _____".
Below is the output when we input our favorite color as Blue

```
What is your favorite color? Blue
Your favorite color is Blue
>>>
```

Exercise

1. Write a program in Python to take the user's name and age as input and display it on the python shell. Hint: You will need to use input(), variables and print().

2. Write a program in Python to take three numbers as input, calculate the sum of the three numbers and print the output. Hint: Create three variables a1, a2 and a3 and print a1+a2+a3

Conditional Statement

Conditional Statements are also known as control statements. They help decide the flow of the program. Sometimes we want a specific block of code to execute only if a certain condition is met. Ex: We take the weather as an input from the user and print "Don't forget your umbrella" if it's rainy or prints "Have a nice day" if it is not.

```
weather = input("Input the weather? ")
if weather == "rainy":
        print("Don't forget your umbrella")
else:
        print("Have a nice day")
```

If the user inputs "rainy", print("Don't forget your umbrella" gets executed and python skips the code inside the else block. If the user inputs something other than "rainy", Python skips the code inside the if block and executes the code in the else block. The general syntax is:

```
if *condition is True* :
        ...... execute this code block ........
```

else:

        .... execute this code block ....

Types of condition

Boolean variable

A boolean variable can have either a value of True or False.

```
boolean = True

if boolean:
    print("The  value is True")
else:
    print("The value is False")
```

First, we declare a boolean variable called 'boolean' and set it True. If 'boolean' is True, we print "The value is True". If it is false, we print "The value is False". Below is the output when 'boolean' is set to True

```
The  value is True
>>> |
```

Comparison operators

The different type of comparison operators supported by Python are:

>   - greater than

<   - less than

== - equal (Note there are two equal signs, a single equal is used to assign values to a variable, two equal signs are used for comparison

!=   - not equal to

>=   - greater than or equal to

<=   - less than or equal to

Comparison can only be made between numbers or string. It is not possible to compare a number to a string. When we take input from the user, we get a string value. If the string contains only numeric characters, we can convert it to an int using int(). Conversion of data types is known as typecasting.

```
number = int (input ("Number? "))

if number > 10:
    print ("{} is greater than 10".format (number))
else:
    print ("{} is not greater than 10".format (number))
```

In the above code, we take an input from the user and convert it to an integer. We then compare it with 10 and print a statement.

If we enter an input of 8, which is less than 10, we get the following output.

```
Number? 8
8 is not greater than 10
>>> |
```

We can also compare strings like the weather example mentioned at the beginning. Below are a few comparison examples in the Python Shell

```
>>> 100 == 101
False
>>> 100 != 101
True
>>> 10 > 9
True
>>> 10 <9
False
>>> 'a' > 'b'
False
>>> 'b' > 'a'
True
>>> 'hello' == 'hello'
True
>>> 'world' == 'WORLD'
False
>>> |
```

Python is case sensitive, as it can be seen in the last example,
'world' != 'WORLD'.

Combination of conditions

Multiple conditions can be combined using the 'and', 'or'
and 'not'.

```
>>> True and True
True
>>> True and False
False
>>> False and False
False
>>> False and True
False
>>> True or True
True
>>> True or False
True
>>> False or True
True
>>> False or False
False
>>> not True
False
>>> not False
True
```

elif keyword

While only one of the if or else code blocks will execute, you may have a case where you want one of many code blocks to execute based on the condition. You can use the elif keyword for such a case. The elif keyword is roughly translated to "else if".

```
number = int (input ("Number? "))

if number > 10:
    print ("{} is greater than 10".format (number))
elif number > 5:
    print ("{} is greater than 5".format (number))
else:
    print ("{} is not greater than 5 or 10".format (number))
```

The above code is similar to the 'number-checker' code we had earlier, but now it also checks if the number is greater than 5. Below is the output when the user inputs 8

```
Number? 8
8 is greater than 5
>>> |
```

Example

1) A function to print the grade based on the mark input by the user

```
def func(mark):
    mark = int(mark)
    if mark >= 90:
        print("Grade A")
    elif mark < 90 and mark >= 80:
        print("Grade B")
    elif mark < 80 and mark >= 70:
        print("Grade C")
    elif mark < 70 and mark >= 60:
        print("Grade D")
    else:
        print("Grade F")


mark = input("Enter the Mark? ")
func(mark)
```

The function 'func' takes a variable mark as a parameter.
It checks for the following conditions:

- If 'mark' is greater than or equal to 90, it prints
  "Grade A"

- If 'mark' is in the range of 80 - 89 (note it's < 90 and
  not <= 90), it prints "Grade B"

- If 'mark' is in the range of 70 - 79, it prints "Grade
  C"

- If 'mark' is in the range of 60 - 69, it prints "Grade
  D"

- If none of the conditions is satisfied, it prints "Garde
  F"

For every input, only one of the conditions is satisfied, and
as a result, only one print statement is executed. Below is
the output for user's input 65

```
Enter the Mark? 65
Grade D
>>> |
```

Since 65 is between 60-69, the third elif condition is satisfied.

Below is the output for user's input 90

```
Enter the Mark? 90
Grade A
>>>
```

Since 90 >=90, the if condition is satisfied, and the if block is executed.

Below is the output when the user's input is 50

```
Enter the Mark? 50
Grade F
>>> |
```

50 is not in any of the above ranges. Therefore, none of the conditions is satisfied, and the else block is executed.

2) A Basic Calculator

```
def Calculator(number1 , number2 , operation):
    number1 = int(number1)
    number2 = int(number2)
    if operation == '+':
        return number1 + number2
    elif operation == '-':
        return number1 - number2
    else:
        return "Operator is not supported"


n1 = input("Enter the first number? ")
n2 = input("Enter the second number? ")
op = input("Enter the operator? ")

print(Calculator(n1,n2,op))
```

The above code takes two numbers and an operator as an input from the user. It returns the sum or difference based on the operator the user inputs. The following checks are performed:

- If the operator is '+', we return the sum of the two numbers
- If the operator is '-', we return the difference between the two numbers
- If any other operator is input, we return an error message

Below is the output when the user inputs 10, 20, +

```
Enter the first number? 10
Enter the second number? 20
Enter the operator? +
30
```

Since the operator is '+', the if condition is executed and
the sum is returned.

Below is the output when the user inputs 20, 10, -

```
Enter the first number? 20
Enter the second number? 10
Enter the operator? -
10
>>> |
```

Since the operator is '-', the elif condition is executed, and
the difference is returned.

Below is the output when the user inputs an invalid
operator

```
Enter the first number? 20
Enter the second number? 10
Enter the operator? /
Operator is not supported
>>> |
```

The operator '/' doesn't satisfy the if or the elif condition,
therefore, the else code block is executed

Exercise

1) Extend the calculator function above to support multiplication and division operators.

2) Write a function which takes two numbers as input from the user and returns "Yes" if number 1 is divisible by number 2 and "No" if it is not. Hint: Use the modulo operator, '%'. It returns the remainder of number1 divided by number2. If it returns 0, it is divisible.

Nested Conditional Statements

In cases when we want multiple conditions to be checked, using keywords 'and' and 'or' makes code hard to read, therefore, we used nested conditional statements. Nested conditional statements are simply if..else blocks inside an if , elif or else block. Below is the general syntax:

```
if *condition is True* :
            if *condition is True* :
                        …… execute this code block
……..

            elif *conditio is True*:
                        ……. execute this code block
……..

            else:
                        …… execute this code block
……..

            else:
……. execute this code block ……..
```

Example

In this example, we are going to take a 4-digit year as an input and check if it is a leap year. Now, this is a little more complicated than we think. We know that every 4 years is a leap year. So that is our first check. So, a year like 1996 would be a leap year. But, every 100 years, there is no leap year. So, 1800 and 1900 are not leap years. Also, there is another exception. Every 400 years, it is not a leap year. So, 1600 and 2000 are not leap years. So, there are 3 checks.

```
def check_leap(year):
    year = int(year)
    leap = False
    if year % 4 == 0:
        leap = True
        if year % 100 == 0:
            leap = False
            if year % 400 == 0:
                leap = True
    return leap

year = input("Enter the year? ")

if check_leap(year):
    print("It is a leap year")
else:
    print("It is not a leap year")
```

The function check_leap takes the year as a parameter and returns True or False based on the conditions. First, we declare a boolean variable 'leap' and initially set it to False. Then we perform the following checks:

- If the year is divisible by 4, we set leap to True and return True. Then we enter the second loop to check if it is divisible by 100.
  - If the year is divisible by 100, we set the leap to False since the year might not be a leap year. If it is divisible by both 4 and 100, we enter the 3rd loop to check if it is divisible by 400.
    - If the year is divisible by 400, it must be a leap year, so we set leap to True and return True.
    - If the year is not divisible by 400, but it is divisible by 100, it is not a leap year. We set leap to False and return False.
  - If the year is not divisible by 100, we return True.
- If it is not, we set it to False since a leap year must be divisible by 4 and return False.

We take the year as input from the user, call the function, passing the input as a parameter, and check if the return value is true or false.

- If check_leap returns True, the year is leap and we print "It is a leap year".
- If the check_leap returns False, the year is not leap, and we print "It is not a leap year".

Below are a few executions of the code:

```
Enter the year? 1992
It is a leap year
>>>

Enter the year? 1995
It is not a leap year
>>>

Enter the year? 1900
It is not a leap year
>>>

Enter the year? 2000
It is a leap year
>>> |
```

As you can see from the above code and results, it accurately calculates the leap year using 3 nested IF statements.

- 1992 is a leap year since it is divisible by 4.
- 1995 is not a leap year since it is not divisible by 4.
- 1900 is not a leap year since it is divisible by both 100 and 4; but not divisible by 400.

- 2000 is a leap year since it is divisible by 4, 100 and 400.

Exercise

1) Write a program that takes in as user input the number of inches of snow, number of inches of ice and the presence of salt. Check if snow day should be declared or not. It is a snow day if there is more than 15 inches of Snow. However, if there is salt, no snow day is given. If there is ice and snow together, snow day is given irrespective of whether salt is present or not.

2) Write a program that takes in a TV program time, TV program type and whether parents are present. Check if children can watch TV or not. Children can watch TV anytime between 6:00 pm and 7:00 pm. After 7, the rating of the tv show will have to be checked. If it's for a general audience and before 10 pm, they can watch TV.   If it's for a mature audience before 10 pm and a parent is present, they can watch it. However, if a parent is not present, they cannot watch it. They cannot watch TV irrespective of the rating and presence of their parents after 10pm.

Loops

Loops in Python are used when we want a block of code to be repeated. We usually set conditions for the block to be repeated, as long as the condition is satisfied the block of code is repeated. As soon as the condition is no longer satisfied, the loop ends and the code block is no longer repeated.

Python has two kinds of loop:

      1) for loop

      2) while loop

FOR loop

A FOR loop is used when we know the number of times, we want the loop to be executed. For loops are also used in arrays, which will be discussed in the next chapter. Below is the syntax for a for loop to repeat a block of code 10 times.

```
for i in range(0,10):
        ........ block of code .........
```

In the above piece of code , the variable 'i' is initially set to 0, and 'i' is incremented by 1 every time the block of code executes. Before executing the block of code , a check is made: if 'i' is less than 10, the loop is executed, if 'i' is greater than or equal to 10 the loop is not executed and Python starts executing the code outside of the loop.

In general, the variable is initially set to the first parameter in range and is incremented by 1 every time the loop is executed until its value reaches the second parameter.

```
for i in range(0,10):
    print(i)
```

In the above code, we print the value of the variable 'i' during each execution of the loop. Below is the output

```
0
1
2
3
4
5
6
7
8
9
>>>
```

After 'i' = 9, 'i' is incremented to 10 and since 'i' is no longer less than 10, we exit the loop.

Example 1

We will write a program which takes an integer as an input from the user and returns the sum of all even numbers between 0 and that number.

```
def sum_even(number):
    number = int(number)
    sum = 0
    for i in range(0,number):
        if i%2 == 0:
            sum = sum + i
    return sum


number = input("Please input the number? ")
print(sum_even(number))
```

The function sum_even takes in a number as a parameter and returns the sum of all the even numbers up to that number, excluding the number. The following steps are performed:

1. We set variable 'sum' to 0
2. A loop is created which starts at 'i' =0 and runs till 'i' = number input by user with increments of 1
3. Inside the loop a check is performed to determine if 'i' is even or not
4. If 'i' is even, we update the value of 'sum' to the 'sum' + i

46

5. Once i is equal to the input number, we exit the loop and return the sum.

Below is the output when input is 10

```
Please input the number? 10
20
>>> |
```

The numbers which are even between 0 and 10 are 2,4,6,8 and 2+4+6+8 = 20. Below is the output when input is 20

```
Please input the number? 20
90
>>>
```

The numbers which are even between 0 and 20 are 2,4,6,8,10,12,14,16,18 and 2+4+6+8+10+12+14+16+18 = 90. Therefore, our code works as expected

Example 2

We will write a function which will print a *n x n* square filled with stars (*).

```
def print_square(number):
    n = int(number)
    for row in range(n):
        for col in range(n):
            print("*", end='')
        print('')

number = input("Please enter the value of n:")
print_square(number)
```

The function print_square takes in a number as a
parameter and prints a
n x n square filled with *.

1. First, we need a loop to iterate through each row of
   the square, this iterator is called "row" and goes
   from 0 to n-1.

   Note: when no starting point provided for range(), it
will start from 0 and go up to n-1

2. Next, we need to iterate through each column, we
   call this iterator col.

3. Using these 2 iterators, we can think of the square
   as an *n x n* table in which we have to fill in each
   block.

4. Now we have to print the "*" for each column in a
   row. We need to ensure that we specify end="
   because otherwise python would move to a new

48

line after every print causing all the * to be on a separate line.

5. After iterating through every column of a row, we need to move to a new line before going to the next row, thus we use print('')

Output for n = 3:

```
Please enter the value of n:3
* * *
* * *
* * *
        .
```

Output for n = 10:

```
Please enter the value of n:10
* * * * * * * * * *
* * * * * * * * * *
* * * * * * * * * *
* * * * * * * * * *
* * * * * * * * * *
* * * * * * * * * *
* * * * * * * * * *
* * * * * * * * * *
* * * * * * * * * *
* * * * * * * * * *
        .
```

While loop

A while loop is used when we do not know the number of times we want the loop to be executed. A while loop keeps on running as long as a predefined condition is True, once False it exits the loop. Below is the general syntax for a while loop

while condition:

.... block of code ....

A for loop can also be written as a while loop. If we want to print the numbers between 0 to 10, excluding 10, below is the code:

```
i = 0

while i<10:
    print(i)
    i = i+1
```

First we set a variable 'i' to 0 and increment it by 1 every time the block of code inside the loop is executed. Before executing the block of code, we check if the value of i is less than 10. If the condition evaluates to True, we execute the code, if it evaluates to False, we exit the loop. Below is the output:

```
0
1
2
3
4
5
6
7
8
9
>>>
```

Like before, when i = 9, the loop is executed, i.e we print i and increment i by 1. When i = 10, the condition evaluates to false and we exit the loop.

Example 1

Below is a function that takes an input from the user and prints it. This keeps on being repeated till the user inputs the word 'exit'.

```
def func():
    status = True
    while status:
        word = input("Enter the word? ")
        if word == 'exit':
            status = False

func()
```

We define a function func to take input from the user and print it to the console repeatedly. We stop once the user inputs 'exit'. First we declare a boolean variable 'status' and set it to True. The while loop keeps on running as long as the boolean variable has a value True

```
Enter the word? test
Enter the word? Loop
Enter the word? Python is cool
Enter the word? Hello world
Enter the word? exit
>>>
```

As you can see, when we input 'test', 'Loop', 'Python is cool', 'Hello world' Python keeps on asking us for input but as soon as we input 'exit', we exit the while loop and the program ends.

Example 2

Below is a function that takes in a number (n) and adds all integer numbers from 1,2 …. N.

```
def add_numbers(n):
    n = int(n)
    total = 0
    counter = 1
    while counter <= n:
        total = total + counter
        counter = counter + 1
    return total

n = input("Please enter value of n: ")
print("Total sum is", add_numbers(n))
```

Counter is the current number being added, starting from 1. Total is the summation of the numbers so far. We increment counter by 1 every iteration to change the number being added, so counter goes 1,2,3... n. When the counter reaches n + 1 the while loop will break, and we return the total at the end.

Output for n = 3, 1 + 2 +3 = 6:

```
Please enter value of n: 3
Total sum is 6
```

Output for n = 7, 1 + 2 + 3 + 4 + 5 + 6 + 7 = 28:

```
Please enter value of n: 7
Total sum is 28
```

Exercise

1) Write a program which takes a number as an input and returns the sum of all odd numbers between 0 and that number

2) Write a program which takes a number and prints the first 10 multiples of that number (excluding the number). So, if we accept 6 as an input, we print:

6 x 1 = 6

6 x 2 = 12

6 x 3 = 18

6 x 4 = 24

6 x 5 = 30

6 x 6 = 36

6 x 7 = 42

6 x 8 = 48

6 x 9 = 54

6 x 10 = 60

3) Make a guessing game.
   a) Create a variable 'guess' and set it to a random integer between 0 and 10 and create a variable 'lives' and initially set it to 3.

b) Take the user's guess as an input, decrement 'lives' by 1 for each wrong guess

c) If player's guess is +/- 2 from the correct answer, print "Hot" else print "Cold"

d) The player has 3 lives. i.e once variable 'lives' is equal to 0, the game is over and the user cannot guess any more

4) Print a n x n square where every odd row is filled with '#" and every even row filled with '#'

Arrays

An array is used to store multiple values together. Imagine you want to store the names of 5 cars, one way would be create10 different variables to store the values. The variables could be 'car1' , 'car2' , 'car3','car4''car5'. Now if you have to print all the names, you'd have to type the print statement 5 times for each car. Now imagine if instead of 5 cars, you are dealing with 100 cars. It will be really tedious.

An array helps us solve this problem. An array in Python is called a List. Below is the syntax for declaring an array:

carNames = ['Toyota' , 'Ford' , 'BMW' , 'Ferrari' , 'Porsche']

The square brackets tells Python that the variable is a list and is expected to store multiple values. Each value in a list is called an element, i.e. 'Toyota' is an element, 'BMW' is an element and so on. Each element in a list has an index, the first element in the list has an index 0. Note that it's not 1, it starts from 0. The last element in our case has an index 4.

Suppose we want to access the element at index x, we use the following syntax

carNames[x]

Not x has to be a valid index, i.e it can not be greater than the total number of elements in the list -1.

```
carNames = [ 'Toyota' , 'Ford' , 'BMW' , 'Ferrari' , 'Porsche']

print('Car number 1 is',carNames[0])
print('Car number 2 is ',carNames[1])
print('Car number 3 is ',carNames[2])
print('Car number 4 is ',carNames[3])
print('Car number 5 is ',carNames[4])
```

Notice how the index is 1 less than the actual position of the element in the list. Below is the output for the print statements.

```
Car number 1 is Toyota
Car number 2 is  Ford
Car number 3 is  BMW
Car number 4 is  Ferrari
Car number 5 is  Porsche
>>>
```

This still doesn't solve the problem of typing multiple print statements. Notice how the index always increments by one, we can use a for loop and set the index as a variable.

```
carNames = [ 'Toyota' , 'Ford' , 'BMW' , 'Ferrari' , 'Porsche']

for i in range(0,5):
    print("Car numebr " , i+1 , " is " , carNames[0])
```

Variable 'i' is initially 0 and the loop executes as long as 'i' is less than 5, i.e 'i' takes the values between 0 and 5 excluding 5. The output for the above code will be similar to the previous output.

There is another way to access all the elements in the list using a for loop.

```
carNames = [ 'Toyota' , 'Ford' , 'BMW' , 'Ferrari' , 'Porsche']

for car in carNames:
    print("Car is " , car)
```

We use the 'in' keyword. The variable car iterates over the list and takes each element's value.

     - During the first execution of the loop, car has the value 'Toyota'

     - During the second execution of the loop, car has the value 'Ford'

     - During the third execution of the loop, car has the value 'BMW'

     and so on.

The loop keeps on executing as long as there are elements present in the list.

A list can have duplicate values and it can have string values , integer values, boolean values , float values or a mix.

```
list1 = [ 1 , 'test' , True , False , 9.1 , 1 ,'test']
for element in list1:
    print("The element is ",element)
```

In the above piece of code, list1 has a mix of different types of variables and duplicate values. Below is the output for the print statement

```
The element is   1
The element is   test
The element is   True
The element is   False
The element is   9.1
The element is   1
The element is   test
>>>
```

Python has many built-in functions for lists and below are a few

1) Length of the List

   The len(list) function returns the length of the list, i.e the number of elements in the list

2) Add element to end of List

   The list.append(value) function lets us add an element to the end of the list

3) Add element to specific index of List

   The list.insert(index , value) function lets us add an element at a specific index within the list

4) Remove last element of the list

The list.pop() function removes the last element of the list

5) Remove a specific value from the list

The list.remove(value) function removes the first occurrence of the value in the list

6) Accessing multiple elements in the list

We can access multiple elements in a list using the ':' operator.

list[0] returns the first element

list[0:4] returns the elements from index 0 to index 3, Note index 4 is not included

list[0:] returns the elements from index 0 till the end of the list

list[2:] return the elements from index 2 till the end of the list

The index -1 refers to the last element of the list , -2 refers to the second last element and so on.

Below various list functions are used in the Python Shell

```
>>> list = [ 1 , 5 , 10 , 90 , 100 , 13 , 15 , 19 , 20 , 10]
>>> len(list)
10
>>> list.append("New Element")
>>> len(list)
11
>>> list
[1, 5, 10, 90, 100, 13, 15, 19, 20, 10, 'New Element']
>>> list.insert(2,"New Elemeent")
>>> len(list)
12
>>> list
[1, 5, 'New Elemeent', 10, 90, 100, 13, 15, 19, 20, 10, 'New Element']
>>> list.pop()
'New Element'
>>> len(list)
11
>>> list.remove(10)
>>> len(list)
10
>>> list
[1, 5, 'New Elemeent', 90, 100, 13, 15, 19, 20, 10]
>>> |
```

1) First, we declare a list with various integer values

2) We use the len function to get the length of the list, which is 10

3) Then we insert a new element to end with the value 'New Element' and print the length of the list. The length increase by 1 as expected and upon printing the length we can see that the new element got inserted to the end of the list

4) We use the .insert() function to insert another element at index 2 and upon printing the list and the length, we see it works as expected.

63

5) Then we try to remove the last element, i.e the element we inserted in step 3.

   The length of the list should be decreased by 1 and print the length and the list confirms that it works as expected.

6) The .remove() function removes the first occurrence of that element, therefore .remove(10) removes the first occurrence of 10 in the list, i.e index 3.

Now we try accessing multiple elements in the list

```
>>> list
[1, 5, 'New Elemeent', 90, 100, 13, 15, 19, 20, 10]
>>> list[0]
1
>>> list[0:]
[1, 5, 'New Elemeent', 90, 100, 13, 15, 19, 20, 10]
>>> list[:4]
[1, 5, 'New Elemeent', 90]
>>> list[2:4]
['New Elemeent', 90]
>>> list[-1]
10
```

1) list[0] prints the first element
2) list[0:] prints all the elements from index 0 till the end
3) list[:4] prints all the elements from index 0 till index 3
4) list[2:4] prints elements at index 2 and 3
5) list[-1] prints the last element

Example 1

We will write a program to take 5 numbers as input from the user and return the sum of all the return all the number incremented by 10

```
input_complete= False
inputs = []
while(not input_complete):
    num = input("Input the number? ")
    inputs.append(int(num) + 10)

    if len(inputs) == 5:
        input_complete = True

print(inputs[0:])
```

First we create a boolean variable and set it to false. We also create an empty list to store the input values. The while loop runs as long as the variable 'input_complete' is False. We keep on taking input from the user, increment it by 10 and add it to the list. We perform a check and set 'input_complete' to False once the length of the list is 5, i.e the user has input 5 elements. We then print the list.

Below is an execution of the program

```
Input the number? 1
Input the number? 2
Input the number? 3
Input the number? 4
Input the number? 5
[11, 12, 13, 14, 15]
>>>
```

Example 2

We will write a program to takes in as many numbers as inputted and prints out their average.

```
input_complete = False
inputs = []
while(not input_complete):
    num = input("Please enter number(enter q to stop):")
    if num == 'q':
        input_complete = True
    else:
        inputs.append(int(num))

print("Input array is ",inputs)

total = 0
count = 0
for i in inputs:
    total = total + i
    count = count + 1

average = total / count
print("Average is: ",average)
```

Similar to the previous example, we create a boolean variable
(*input_complete*) and an array(*inputs*) and use a while loop to get the
inputs, but this time the while loop will stop when we enter the letter 'q'.
After getting all the inputs, we declare a variable *total* to find the sum of
all the inputs and count to track the number of total inputs. We do this
by using a for loop and iterating through each element in the inputs
array. Finally to get the average we just divide the total by count.

```
Please enter number(enter q to stop):2
Please enter number(enter q to stop):3
Please enter number(enter q to stop):5
Please enter number(enter q to stop):4
Please enter number(enter q to stop):q
Input array is   [2, 3, 5, 4]
Average is:   3.5
>>> |
```

Example 3

This time we will write a function which takes in an array and returns the maximum value in the array.

```
def find_max(inputs):
    max_value = inputs[0]
    for item in inputs:
        if item > max_value:
            max_value = item

    return max_value

maximum = find_max([1,3,9,200,6,-10])
print("Max in array is: ", maximum)
```

First we set max_value to the first element in the array. This is temporary. Next we iterate through each element in the array and check if that element is greater than the max we set, if so it will set that value as the new max. Once it has iterated through the entire array, max_value should contain the absolute max in the array.

For the given array [1, 3, 9, 200, 6, -10], output is:

```
Max in array is:    200
>>>
```

Exercise

Take a student's marks in 5 different subjects as input and print the average of all the marks. Also find the minimum and maximum subject mark.

1) Create a list that stores the months of the year. The user can input the number of the month and the function should link the number with the actual month using the array. Then print out the relevant month in the array.

2) Create a list of names and check if there are any 2 names that are the same. Return a boolean (True or False) depending on whether there is a same name or not.

Having Fun with Strings

A string is an array of characters, i.e. 'Hello' can be represented as ['H','e','l','l','o']. Therefore we can use all the previously discussed array functions on strings as well.

```
string = "Hello"

for character in string:
    print(character)
```

Below is the output

```
H
e
l
l
o
>>> |
```

Below are a few functions that are helpful while dealing with strings.

Split

The .split() function takes in a value and splits the string using the value as a seperator into an array of smaller strings.

```
>>> s = "Python is cool"
>>> s.split(' ')
['Python', 'is', 'cool']
>>> s = 'a,b,c,d,e,f,g'
>>> s.split(',')
['a', 'b', 'c', 'd', 'e', 'f', 'g']
>>> |
```

In the first instance, we split the string using space as a separator and in the second instance we split the string using a comma as a separator

Is functions

isalnum() - Returns True if all characters in the string are alphanumeric

isalpha() - Returns True if all characters in the string are in the alphabet

islower() - Returns True if all characters in the string are lower case

isnumeric() - Returns True if all characters in the string are numeric

isupper() - Returns True if all characters in the string are in upper case

```
>>> 'Hello'.isalnum()
True
>>> 'Hello!!!'.isalnum()
False
>>> 'Hello'.isalpha()
True
>>> 'Hello'.isnumeric()
False
>>> '12345'.isnumeric()
True
>>> 'H3110'.isnumeric()
False
>>> 'Hello'.islower()
False
>>> 'hello'.islower()
True
>>> 'HELLO'.isupper()
True
>>> |
```

1) 'Hello' only contains alphabets therefore isalnum returns True

2) 'Hello!!' contains exclamation marks therefore isalnum returns False

3) 'Hello' contains only alphabets therefore isalpha returns True

4) 'Hello' contains alphabets and not digits, therefore isnumeric returns False

5) '12345' contains numbers therefore isnumeric returns True

6) 'H3ll0' contains alphabets therefore isnumeric returns False

7) 'Hello' contains an upper case character therefore islower returns False

8) 'Hello' contains all lower case characters therefore islower returns True

9) 'HELLO' contains all upper case characters
   therefore isupper returns True

Strip

lstrip() removes trailing spaces in the beginning of the
string , rstrip() removes trailing spaces at the end of the
string, strip() removes trailing spaces from the beginning
and end of the string

```
>>> s = '        Hi        '
>>> len(s.lstrip())
9
>>> len(s.rstrip())
9
>>> len(s.strip())
2
>>> |
```

's' is a string variable with 7 spaces at the beginning and 7
at the end. Therefore the total length is 16.
1) lstrip() removes the first 7 space characters
   therefore length is 9
2) rstrip() removes the last 7 space characters
   therefore length is 9
3) strip() removes the first 7 and last 7 therefore the
   length is 2

Case change

upper() converts all characters to uppercase, lower() converts all characters to lowercase and swapcase converts lowercase characters to uppercase and uppercase characters to lowercase.

```
>>> 'HeLLo'.lower()
'hello'
>>> 'HeLLo'.upper()
'HELLO'
>>> 'HeLLo'.swapcase()
'hEllO'
>>> |
```

Concatenation

The + operator can be used to join strings.

```
>>> s1 = 'Hello'
>>> s2 = 'World'
>>> s1+s2
'HelloWorld'
>>> |
```

Only two strings can be concatenated, you cannot use the + operator to concatenate a string and an integer. You could however convert the integer to a string using str() and concatenate it to another string.

```
>>> 'Hi' + 2
Traceback (most recent call last):
  File "<pyshell#23>", line 1, in <module>
    'Hi' + 2
TypeError: can only concatenate str (not "int") to str
>>> 'Hi' + str(2)
'Hi2'
>>> |
```

As you can see 'Hi' + 2 gives us an error since 2 is an integer but using str(2) converter it to a string and the result is 'HI2'

Join

The join function is used to create a string from a list. It accepts a value which can be used as a separator and joins all the elements in the list to form a string. Make sure all elements in the list are of type string or converted to a string

```
>>> ''.join(['Test' , 'Join' , 'Function' , 'Hello' , 'Wordl'])
'TestJoinFunctionHelloWordl'
>>> ' '.join(['Test' , 'Join' , 'Function' , 'Hello' , 'Wordl'])
'Test Join Function Hello Wordl'
>>> ','.join(['Test' , 'Join' , 'Function' , 'Hello' , 'Wordl'])
'Test,Join,Function,Hello,Wordl'
>>> |
```

In the first case we do not pass any separator and it joins the strings without any spaces or a separator. In the second instance we pass a space as the separator and therefore the result has spaces between the words. In the thor instance we pass a comma and words have a comma between them.

Find

The find functions returns the index of the first occurrence of the word in a string. If the word is not found it returns -1.

```
>>> "Hello World".find("Hello")
0
>>> "Hello World".find("World")
6
>>> "Hello World".find("world")
-1
>>> "Hello World".find("Python")
-1
>>> |
```

In the first instance we try to find "Hello" in the string "Hello World" and it returns 0 since 0 is the start index where it finds the first occurrence of 'Hello". Similarly, in the second instance, it returns 6 since 6 is the start index. Note that Python is case sensitive and therefore when we try to search for 'world' it returns -1. It also returns -1 when we try to search for 'Python' since it is not present in 'Hello World'

Replace

The replace function is used to replace a string with another string as can be seen in the example below

```
>>> "Hello World".replace("o" , "2")
'Hell2 W2rld'
>>> "Hello World".replace("Hello" ,"*")
'* World'
>>> |
```

In the first instance we replace all occurrence of letter 0 with "2" and in the second instance we replace "Hello" with "*"

Exercise

1) Write a program that finds how many times a particular string occurs within a bigger string that is input.

2) Write a program that takes in a string that includes a name and marks separated by commas. Split the string and calculate the average of the marks. The return value should be the name followed by the average.

3) Write a program that takes in a name and address and checks if the address contains the text 'Atlanta'. Have a counter that increments every time this happens; and at the end of the program print out the number of people from Atlanta.

Math Functions

The Math Library provides us access to some common math functions and constants in Python. To use the math library we need to import it by typing "import math" in our python file. To access any of its functions or constants, we need to precede them by 'math.'

Constants

```
import math

print(math.pi)
print(math.e)
```

Math.pi returns the constant pi and math.e returns the value for constant e

```
3.141592653589793
2.718281828459045
>>>
```

exp() Function

The exp() function can be used to calculate the power of e.

```
>>> math.exp(10)
22026.465794806718
>>> math.exp(5)
148.4131591025766
>>>
```

log() Function

This function returns the logarithm of the specified number. The natural logarithm is computed with respect to the base e. The following example demonstrates the usage of this function:

```
>>> math.log(10)
2.302585092994046
>>> math.log(1)
0.0
>>>
```

It can also be used as log(x,y) where y is base.

```
>>> math.log(100,10)
2.0
>>> math.log(10,3)
2.095903274289385
>>> |
```

Arithmetic Functions

Arithmetic functions are used to perform mathematical operations. Some of the most common arithmetic functions are discussed below:

- ceil(a): returns the ceiling value of the specified number.
- fabs(a): returns the absolute value of the specified number.
- floor(a): returns the floor value of the specified number.
- gcd(a, b): returns the greatest common divisor of a and b.
- pow(a,b): returns result of first number raised to the second number
- sqrt(a): returns the square root of the specified number.

```
>>> import math
>>> math.ceil(3.5)
4
>>> math.floor(3.5)
3
>>> math.fabs(-3.5)
3.5
>>> math.gcd(10,20)
10
>>> math.pow(2,3)
8.0
>>> math.sqrt(9)
3.0
>>> |
```

Conclusion

Thank you for downloading this book. I hope you have enjoyed the content and applied everything that is included in this book. This is just a first step to get you started and enjoying programming.

There's a lot more to come. I will come out with books that are a little more advanced in the future.

If you'd like one-on-one training as well, you can contact me at abiprod.pty.ltd@gmail.com

In the mean time, if you're interested, you can check out these books below:

Python Crash Course by Eric Matthes

Learning Python by Mark Lutz

Python Programming by John Zelle

If you'd like a similar basic introduction to JavaScript, you can try out my book below:

Coding for Kids in JavaScript by Bob Mather

CPSIA information can be obtained
at www.ICGtesting.com
Printed in the USA
LVHW020040061120
670806LV00008B/313